CHECKERBOARD SOCIAL STUDIES LIBRARY

DEFENDING THE NATION

Defending the Nation

THE COAST GUARD

John Hamilton
ABDO Publishing Company

visit us at
www.abdopublishing.com

Published by ABDO Publishing Company, 4940 Viking Drive, Edina, Minnesota 55435.
Copyright © 2007 by Abdo Consulting Group, Inc. International copyrights reserved in all
countries. No part of this book may be reproduced in any form without written permission from
the publisher. The Checkerboard Library™ is a trademark and logo of ABDO Publishing
Company.

Printed in the United States.

Cover Photos: front, U.S. Coast Guard; back, U.S. Air Force
Interior Photos: Bridgeman Art Library pp. 8-9; Corbis pp. 1, 4, 16-17; U.S. Air Force p. 23;
     U.S. Coast Guard pp. 5, 10, 11, 13, 14, 15, 17, 19, 20, 21, 25, 26, 28-29

Series Coordinator: Megan M. Gunderson
Editors: Rochelle Baltzer, Megan M. Gunderson
Art Direction & Cover Design: Neil Klinepier

Library of Congress Cataloging-in-Publication Data

Hamilton, John, 1959-
  The Coast Guard / John Hamilton.
     p. cm. -- (Defending the nation)
  Includes index.
  ISBN-13: 978-1-59679-755-0
  ISBN-10: 1-59679-755-X
  1. United States. Coast Guard--Juvenile literature. I. Title II. Series: Hamilton, John, 1959- .
Defending the nation.

VG53.H36 2007
363.28'60973--dc22

2005035426

Contents

The U.S. Coast Guard

The U.S. Coast Guard emblem

The U.S. Coast Guard is the oldest continuous seagoing service in the United States. Today, it is part of the U.S. Department of Homeland Security. The coast guard has more than 40,000 active-duty members. This makes it the smallest branch of the U.S. armed forces.

Despite its size, the coast guard has many important missions. It rescues people in trouble on water, such as fishers whose boats are sinking. The coast guard protects U.S. harbors from **terrorist** attacks. And, it stops criminals from **smuggling** illegal drugs into U.S. ports. The coast guard also maintains navigational aids, such as **buoys** and channel markers. And, it responds to **environmental** disasters such as oil spills.

The U.S. Coast Guard may be smaller than other U.S. military branches. But its motto, *Semper paratus*, is Latin for "always ready." The brave men and women of the U.S. Coast Guard are proud of the important jobs they perform to keep Americans safe.

Admiral Thad W. Allen became commandant of the U.S. Coast Guard on May 25, 2006.

4

Timeline

1790 - On August 4, the Revenue Cutter Service was founded as part of the U.S. Department of the Treasury.

1871 - The U.S. Lifesaving Service was established.

1914 - The Revenue Cutter Service was put in charge of the International Ice Patrol.

1915 - Congress combined the Revenue Cutter Service and the U.S. Lifesaving Service to create the U.S. Coast Guard.

1939 - The Federal Lighthouse Service became part of the U.S. Coast Guard; the Coast Guard Auxiliary was founded through the Coast Guard Reserve Act of 1939.

1941 - The Coast Guard Reserve and Auxiliary Act of February 19, 1941, established the Coast Guard Reserve as a separate service.

1942 - The Bureau of Marine Inspection and Navigation became part of the U.S. Coast Guard.

1967 - The U.S. Department of Transportation took control of the U.S. Coast Guard.

2003 - The U.S. Coast Guard became part of the U.S. Department of Homeland Security.

Fun Facts

• In times past, the coast guard operated the many lighthouses dotting the shores of America's most dangerous waters. But today, the only U.S. lighthouse manned by the coast guard is Boston Light, near Boston, Massachusetts.

• On average, the U.S. Coast Guard saves 15 lives each day. And, it helps more than 100 other individuals in need of assistance.

History of the Coast Guard

The U.S. Coast Guard developed over a long period of time. Over the past 200 years, five separate government agencies combined to form today's U.S. Coast Guard. These agencies include the Revenue Cutter Service, the Federal Lighthouse Service, the Steamboat Inspection Service, the Bureau of Marine Inspection and Navigation, and the U.S. Lifesaving Service.

The coast guard traces its earliest roots to the Revenue Cutter Service. Secretary of the Treasury Alexander Hamilton recommended the service's formation. It began under the control of the U.S. Department of the Treasury on August 4, 1790. The U.S. Coast Guard still considers this date its birthday.

The same year, Congress **disbanded** the Continental navy. So until the U.S. Navy was created in 1798, the Revenue Cutter Service was the only naval force available to the United States. This vital service began with ten ships called cutters.

In these early days, the Revenue Cutter Service's main responsibility was law enforcement. It made sure ships carrying goods from foreign lands paid a tax called a tariff. The service also **intercepted** ships carrying slaves and protected America's shores from pirates and **smugglers**.

Early coast guard cutters were vital to America's protection. Today, modern cutters continue to provide national security.

Coast guard rescue efforts during Hurricane Katrina in 2005

The U.S. Lifesaving Service was established in 1871 to save shipwrecked sailors. In 1915, Congress combined the Revenue Cutter Service with the Lifesaving Service. This act created the U.S. Coast Guard.

Then in 1939, the Federal Lighthouse Service merged into the coast guard. This service maintained and operated lighthouses on America's shores. And in 1942, the Bureau of Marine Inspection and Navigation also transferred to the coast guard's control.

The coast guard has been called upon regularly in times of war. In fact, the cutter *Harriet Lane* fired the first shots at sea during the American **Civil War**. During **World War I**, several coast guard cutters served as escorts for other ships. They protected the ships while they traveled from one place to another. During the war, a German submarine destroyed USCGC *Tampa*. The *Tampa* had been acting as an escort between Gibraltar and Great Britain.

In 1967, control of the coast guard transferred from the Department of the Treasury to the U.S. Department of Transportation. But after the **terrorist** attacks of September 11, 2001, control of the coast guard changed again. In 2003, the coast guard became part of the new Department of Homeland Security.

On August 28, 2005, powerful Hurricane Katrina roared ashore in Louisiana, Mississippi, and Alabama. Thousands of people were killed or injured. In New Orleans, Louisiana, a levee system failed. The failure of these barriers sent the waters of Lake Pontchartrain pouring into city streets. Thousands of homes and businesses were flooded. And, many people were trapped by the rising waters.

At the time of the hurricane, the coast guard chief of staff was Vice Admiral Thad W. Allen. On September 9, he was named principal federal official. Allen directed the coast guard's search and rescue efforts.

The U.S. Coast Guard was prepared to respond quickly to the disaster. It rescued more than 33,500 people. That was

Thad W. Allen was promoted to admiral in 2006

six times the number of people it saved nationwide in 2004. The coast guard also helped in many other ways. It provided aid and comfort to hurricane victims. Stranded hurricane survivors were relieved they could count on the coast guard for help.

Coast Guard Missions

The U.S. Coast Guard is responsible for numerous missions and tasks. Each mission is a critical part of its duty to protect the United States. The spirit of helping those in need is very important to coast guard members. The U.S. Coast Guard is responsible for 361 ports and more than 95,000 nautical miles (175,000 km) of coastline.

Maritime safety is one of the coast guard's oldest and most important missions. This mission includes search and rescue functions. Almost every day, someone in U.S. waters needs rescuing. It might be a recreational boater, a fisher, or even someone whose aircraft has crashed into the sea.

The coast guard is equipped to work both near the shore and over the ocean. It uses boats and helicopters to help those in need. Specially trained rescue jumpers leap from helicopters into dangerous waters to save stranded boaters!

Besides conducting search and rescue missions, the coast guard promotes boating safety. It inspects ships to make sure they are properly registered and carry the right safety equipment. This includes personal flotation devices, fire extinguishers, and flares.

Having proper life preservers is an important part of boating safety.

Aviation survival technicians are rescue swimmers. They train continuously to prepare for dangerous rescue situations.

As part of its maritime mobility mission, the coast guard maintains a system of **beacons** and **buoys** in U.S. waterways. These aids to navigation are much like the street signs car drivers use. Boats use navigational aids such as channel markers and fog signals. Together with detailed charts and maps, these tools help boats stay out of danger.

Besides marking unsafe waters, the coast guard also keeps waterways open and safe. It regulates the operation of drawbridges to manage traffic between cars and ships. And in the winter, the coast guard uses large icebreaker ships to keep important waterways clear of ice.

The coast guard is also responsible for patrolling the North Atlantic Ocean. It received this duty two years after the HMS *Titanic* struck an iceberg and sank

Coast guard aircraft, such as this C-130, patrol the North Atlantic during iceberg season. This lasts from January to September.

in 1912. Today, the International Ice Patrol uses aircraft to locate and warn ships about dangerous icebergs.

In addition, the coast guard is responsible for protecting natural resources. Marine pollution happens almost daily. When a ship wrecks, the coast guard tries to contain and clean up any pollution it causes. It attempts to trap oil or other chemicals before they wash up on nearby shores. The coast guard also helps state officials determine the amount of damage.

The coast guard uses protective booms, or barriers, to keep oil spills from spreading.

All ships must provide notice before entering American waters. As part of its maritime security mission, the coast guard conducts inspections of suspicious ships.

The coast guard works closely with other federal law enforcement agencies, such as the U.S. Customs Service. Together, they perform **interdiction** missions. Coast guard helicopters, airplanes, and ships are **aggressive** in stopping the flow of illegal drugs into the United States. Each year, drug interdiction missions seize billions of dollars worth of illegal substances at sea.

Some interdiction missions are related to **immigration**. Each year, thousands of migrants try to illegally enter the United States by boat. The

The coast guard aims to prevent loss of life by intercepting overloaded migrant vessels in U.S. waters.

coast guard **intercepts** them and returns them to their home countries. It also rescues migrants when their boats overturn or sink.

Today, coast guard responsibilities largely focus on stopping **terrorism**. Beginning in 2002, several coast guard patrol boats were sent to work in the Persian Gulf. Their mission was to prevent illegal goods from being **smuggled** into Iraq. Coast guard vessels also helped provide security for ports, as well as coastal defense.

Among other duties, the coast guard has helped patrol Iraqi waters for oil smugglers.

Coast Guard Assets

The boats, airplanes, and helicopters that the coast guard uses are called assets. The coast guard uses all of its assets together to perform its varied missions.

Coast guard cutters are large ships. To be called a cutter, a ship must be at least 65 feet (20 m) long. A crew can live aboard these ships.

High Endurance Cutters are 378 feet (115 m) long. They are so big that helicopters can land on them! They perform many kinds of missions and operate on oceans throughout the world.

The U.S. Coast Guard's largest ship is the 420-foot (128-m) icebreaker USCGC *Healy*. This cutter is designed to crack through polar ice that is more than 4 feet (1 m) thick. And, it is large enough to house more than 140 people. This includes up to 50 scientists who can live on board and study the Arctic **environment**.

Coast guard vessels shorter than 65 feet (20 m) are called boats. They operate near shores or on rivers. Coast guard boats include motor lifeboats and inflatable boats. They also include high-speed pursuit boats used for chasing drug **smugglers**.

As part of the Department of Homeland Security, the coast guard has been patrolling the Washington, D.C., area using rigid-hull inflatable boats.

U.S. Coast Guard assets include more than 200 aircraft. Just like coast guard ships, these assets are used for a variety of missions. But, their main duties are law enforcement and search and rescue.

HC-130 Hercules

The HC-130 Hercules is a long-range aircraft. It can fly more than 5,000 miles (8,000 km) at a time. And, it can fly for up to 14 hours. It is a fixed-wing airplane, which means its wings do not move. The HC-130 has a wingspan of more than 132 feet (40 m). It uses four large turboprop engines. The coast guard uses the HC-130 aircraft for **surveillance**.

The coast guard uses the HH-60 Jayhawk helicopter for search and rescue missions. Rescue swimmers can jump from it to save people stranded in the water. The HH-60 is 65 feet (20 m) long. Its blades span 54 feet (16 m). It cannot fly as far as the HC-130. But, an HH-60 can land on coast guard cutters.

A rescue swimmer jumping from an HH-60 Jayhawk

Organization

The U.S. Coast Guard is organized in a hierarchy similar to the other military branches. This means there are different levels of authority and responsibility. Some people **enlist** in the coast guard directly out of high school. Others join the coast guard as officers after learning special leadership and management skills.

The head of the U.S. military is the president of the United States. He or she is called the commander in chief. The highest position within the U.S. Coast Guard is that of commandant. Below the commandant are the rest of the officer ranks. Enlisted members are also organized by rank.

The coast guard uses nearly the same ranking system as the U.S. Navy. An enlistee can rise to the rank of master chief petty officer of the coast guard. And with proper qualifications, he or she may apply to become an officer. Qualifications include college courses, four or more years of service, and a rank of petty officer second class or above.

Ranks

Members of the U.S. Coast Guard are organized in a hierarchy by rank. A rank is a level of responsibility.

Officer Ranks

Ensign (O-1)

Lieutenant Junior Grade (O-2)

Lieutenant (O-3)

Lieutenant Commander (O-4)

Commander (O-5)

Captain (O-6)

Rear Admiral Lower Half (O-7)

Rear Admiral Upper Half (O-8)

Vice Admiral (O-9)

Admiral (O-10)

Fleet Admiral

Warrant Officer Ranks

Chief Warrant Officer 2 (W-2)

Chief Warrant Officer 3 (W-3)

Chief Warrant Officer 4 (W-4)

W-2

W-3

W-4

Enlisted Ranks

Seaman Recruit (E-1)

Seaman Apprentice (E-2)

Seaman (E-3)

Petty Officer Third Class (E-4)

Petty Officer Second Class (E-5)

Petty Officer First Class (E-6)

Chief Petty Officer (E-7)

Senior Chief Petty Officer (E-8)

Master Chief Petty Officer (E-9)

Fleet/Command Master Chief Petty Officer (E-9)

Master Chief Petty Officer of the Coast Guard (E-9)

O-1

O-5

O-10

E-3

E-4

E-6

E-9

The letter and number next to each rank indicates a person's pay grade.

Coast Guard Reserve

The U.S. Coast Guard has a reserve force like those of the other four military branches. A reserve force is part of a military branch. But, it is only called to active duty when extra help is needed.

Besides a typical reserve force, the coast guard also has the Coast Guard Auxiliary. The Coast Guard Auxiliary was founded through the Coast Guard Reserve Act of 1939. Today, there are more than 30,000 **civilians** in the auxiliary. These volunteers wear uniforms similar to members of the coast guard or the Coast Guard Reserve. But, they do not have ranks.

Still, auxiliary members assist the coast guard in every mission except law enforcement and military operations. Their main focus is promoting safety. Auxiliary members provide public education courses about marine safety. And, they help conduct search and rescue missions.

The Coast Guard Reserve and Auxiliary Act of February 19, 1941, established the Coast Guard Reserve as a separate service.

Coast Guard Auxiliary members are a vital part of the coast guard's success.

The reserve forces train one weekend a month plus two weeks a year. Unlike the auxiliary members, reservists are called upon for all varieties of coast guard missions. Outside the reserve, they pursue **civilian** jobs or schooling.

Joining the Coast Guard

To join the U.S. Coast Guard, a person must be a U.S. citizen between the ages of 17 and 27. And, he or she must have graduated from high school. An applicant can be married, but cannot have more than two children or dependents. He or she must also pass a

military medical exam and a written test. Most important, a candidate must want to serve the public on or around the water.

Enlisted coast guard candidates attend an eight-week boot camp. This tough training course is located at the U.S. Coast Guard Training Center in Cape May, New Jersey. The course teaches valuable skills, including seamanship, weapon use, and first aid. Training is both mentally and physically challenging.

There are several ways to become a U.S. Coast Guard officer. High school graduates can attend the Coast Guard Academy in New London, Connecticut. There, they receive leadership and technical training. Each graduate leaves with a college degree and a rank of ensign. Then, they must serve in the coast guard for at least five years.

People who already have a college degree from another school can also become officers. To do this, they join the Coast Guard Officer Candidate School. This 17-week officer-training program is also located in New London.

All U.S. Coast Guard Academy cadets serve on the Eagle. *This 295-foot (90-m) training ship holds about 150 students.*

The Future of the Coast Guard

Throughout its history, the U.S. Coast Guard has enjoyed numerous successes. But, for many years it has struggled with small budgets and aging equipment. The coast guard's recent missions assisting the war against **terrorism** have resulted in some increased funding. But, its aging **fleet** of ships and aircraft still needs **upgrading**.

The coast guard recently began the Integrated Deepwater System (IDS) Program. The IDS Program is a way of upgrading coast guard assets in a less expensive and more **efficient** way. The coast guard will be adding new ships, aircraft, and communications equipment similar to those used by the U.S. Navy.

Once the project is complete, the coast guard will be better able to perform its missions. The system will also help the coast guard work more closely with the navy. By using the same types of assets, conducting missions together and performing repairs will be easier.

Because of the coast guard's varied missions, it has always had much contact with the American public. Now that it has increased overseas missions, the coast guard works closely with foreign citizens as well. As the men and women of the U.S. Coast Guard perform their duties, they will continue to set a good example for others. In doing so, they will help create goodwill between nations.

The coast guard used the HH-65 Dolphin helicopter in 2003 in Iraq. Now, these helicopters are being updated as part of the IDS Program.

Glossary

aggressive - displaying hostility.

beacon - a signal used for guidance.

buoy (BOO-ee) - a floating object used to mark a water hazard such as rocks or shallow water.

civil war - a war between groups in the same country. The United States of America and the Confederate States of America fought a civil war from 1861 to 1865.

civilian - of or relating to something nonmilitary.

disband - to break up something that is organized.

efficient - wasting little time or energy.

enlist - to join the armed forces voluntarily. An enlistee is a person who enlists for military service.

environment - all the surroundings that affect the growth and well-being of a living thing.

fleet - a group of ships and airplanes under one command.

immigration - entry into another country to live. A person who immigrates is called an immigrant.

intercept - to interrupt the progress of something before it arrives at its destination, usually secretly.

interdiction - of or relating to forbidding, damaging, destroying, or cutting off something.

Glossary

smuggle - to import or export something secretly and often illegally. A person who smuggles is called a smuggler.

surveillance - to watch over someone's activities.

terrorism - the use of terror, violence, or threats to frighten people into action. A person who commits an act of terrorism is called a terrorist.

upgrade - to increase or improve.

World War I - from 1914 to 1918, fought in Europe. Great Britain, France, Russia, the United States, and their allies were on one side. Germany, Austria-Hungary, and their allies were on the other side.

Web Sites

To learn more about the U.S. Coast Guard, visit ABDO Publishing Company on the World Wide Web at **www.abdopublishing.com**. Web sites about the U.S. Coast Guard are featured on our Book Links page. These links are routinely monitored and updated to provide the most current information available.

Index